BEI GRIN MACHT SICH IHR WISSEN BEZAHLT

- Wir veröffentlichen Ihre Hausarbeit,
  Bachelor- und Masterarbeit

- Ihr eigenes eBook und Buch -
  weltweit in allen wichtigen Shops

- Verdienen Sie an jedem Verkauf

Jetzt bei www.GRIN.com hochladen und kostenlos publizieren

Bibliografische Information der Deutschen Nationalbibliothek:

Die Deutsche Bibliothek verzeichnet diese Publikation in der Deutschen National-
bibliografie; detaillierte bibliografische Daten sind im Internet über http://dnb.d-
nb.de/ abrufbar.

Impressum:

Copyright © 2006 GRIN Verlag, Open Publishing GmbH
Druck und Bindung: Books on Demand GmbH, Norderstedt Germany
ISBN: 978-3-668-15809-2

Dieses Buch bei GRIN:

http://www.grin.com/de/e-book/109925/biographie-und-werke-des-heroic-fantasy-
art-zeichners-luis-royo

Sabrin Byaah

Biographie und Werke des "Heroic-Fantasy-Art"-Zeichners Luis Royo

GRIN Verlag

GRIN - Your knowledge has value

Der GRIN Verlag publiziert seit 1998 wissenschaftliche Arbeiten von Studenten, Hochschullehrern und anderen Akademikern als eBook und gedrucktes Buch. Die Verlagswebsite www.grin.com ist die ideale Plattform zur Veröffentlichung von Hausarbeiten, Abschlussarbeiten, wissenschaftlichen Aufsätzen, Dissertationen und Fachbüchern.

Besuchen Sie uns im Internet:

http://www.grin.com/

http://www.facebook.com/grincom

http://www.twitter.com/grin_com

Handout:

LUIS ROYO
(GEBOREN 1954)

„WENN DU DICH ZERSTREUST UND SO WIEDER NEU ERSCHAFFST,
SCHAFFST DU NICHT DAS, WAS ES NICHT GIBT, DU ERBRICHST NUR DAS,
WAS DU GEGESSEN HAST UND WAS IN DIR IST, UND DAS ERBROCHENE,
DAS DU AUF DEM BODEN (GEMEINT IST PAPIER) ZURÜCKLÄSST,
HAT WENIG ZU TUN MIT DEM GEGESSENEN."
LUIS ROYO

SABRIN BYAAH
KL. 1.1
WWW.LUISROYO.COM

20.02.2006
LUIS ROYO

Bücher:

- 1992 Women
- 1994 Malefic
- 1996 Secrets
- 1998 III Millennium
- 1999 Dreams
- 1999 Prohibited Book
- 2001 Evolution
- 2001 Prohibited Book II
- 2002 Conceptions I
- 2003 Prohibited Book III
- 2003 Conceptions II
- 2004 Prohibited Sketchbook

Comicalben:

- Circulus-Sataka
- Desfase

Postkartenset:

- Artist's Choice
- Forbidden Universe
- From Fantasy to Reality
- Millennium
- Secret Desires
- The Art of Heavy Metal
- The Best of Royo

Mappen:

- III Millennium
- Tattoos
- Warm Winds

Anderes:

- Poster
- The Black Tarot
- Striptease Postcard Collection #1
- CD-Cover
- Kalender
- T-Shirts
- Mouse-pads

Eigenes Referat:

Luis Royo

Luis Royo wurde 1954 in Olalla, Teruel in Spanien, geboren. Später zog er mit seiner Familie nach Zaragoza, wo er Bautechnik und später Malerei und Innenarchitektur studierte. Während der 68`er Jahre gab es viele Ausstellungen seiner Bilder, die v.a. soziale Themen als Gegenstand hatten.

Mit 24 Jahren wurde er Comic- Strip Zeichner und bereits 5 Jahre später ein bekannter Illustrator. Er designte viele verschiedene Cover für PC-Games, Videos und CD's. Hauptsächlich für Hardrockbands, wie z.B. Belzebú, Zeitreisen und Black-Flight. 2 Jahre später wurde sein erstes Comic-Album vom Verlag Rambla-Serie veröffentlicht.

1992 schaffte er den weltweiten Durchbruch als Illustrator und Comicbuch-Autor, mit seinem Artbook: WOMEN. Nach dem Erfolg von WOMEN interessierten sich viele weitere Herausgeber, u.a. Doubleday, Pocket Books, Ballantine, Nal usw. für seine Mitarbeit in ihren Verlagen. Sein 3. Artbook SECRETS, in dem er die Geschichte „Die Schöne und das Biest" in einer adaptierten Version erzählt, wurde nur in englisch-sprachigen Ländern verkauft. Noch im gleichen Jahr gewann er den „Silver Award SPECTRUM III for Fantastic Art".

Einige Zeit später wurde vom Heavy Metall Verlag eine Postkartenserie ROYO SECRET DESIRE herausgegeben. 2004 wurden seine bisher letzten Arbeiten veröffentlicht – PROHIBITED SKETCHBOOK und Tarotkarten, THE LABYRINTH.

Ein Teil der Faszination, die von Royo's Bilder ausgeht, liegt in der Darstellung von Gegensätzen, wie Angst und Schrecken, Tod und Verfall, Liebe und Hass, Schönheit und Abscheu, Monster und Maschinen. Bis heute sind seine Arbeiten als Illustrator, Autor und Comic-Strip-Zeichner sehr gefragt.

Die Darstellung von Gewalt in seinen Bildern ist nicht idealisierend, sondern ein Ausdruck von Realität in einer aggressiven Welt:

Zitat Royo: „Ich glaube, ich könnte nicht mal einer Fliege was zu Leide tun. Aber ich mag es zu provozieren, zu beunruhigen."

Bücher

1992 WOMEN

Women war sein 1. Artbook, in dem seine besten Illustartionen beinhaltet waren. Schnell erkennt man, dass er eine große Vorliebe für den weiblichen Körper hat.

1994 MALEFIC

In Malefic enthüllt er seine dunkle und wilde Seite. Seine Bilder beschreiben eine fantastische irreale Welt, nicht nur in Bildern, sondern auch in Stories und differenzierten Charakteren. Zum 1. Mal enthält eines seiner Artbooks auch Skizzen und Kommentare zu seinen Illustrationen.

1998 III MILLENIUM

In Millenium gibt er Einblick in seine Vorstellung vom Ende des Jahrtausends. Seine Landschaften wirken sehr kalt und düster, die Wahl der Farben und Szenarien stellte etwas bis Dahin völlig Neues dar.

1999 PROHIBITED BOOK I

Prohibited Book – das verbotene Buch - ist ein sehr provokatives Werk, in dem seine tiefsten Leidenschaften und verborgensten Begierden wiedergespiegelt werden.

2002 CONCEPTIONS I

In diesem Artbook findet man seine besten Skizzen und unvollendeten Werke wieder.

Infomaterial:

Wenn du dich zerstreust und so wieder neu erschaffst,
schaffst du nicht das, was es nicht gibt, du erbrichst nur das,
was du gegessen hast und was in dir ist, und das Erbrochene,
das du auf dem Boden (gemeint ist Papier) zurückläßt,
hat wenig zu tun mit dem Gegessenen.
Luis Royo

Luis Royo wurde 1954 in Cutanda, Teruel, geboren und ist weltweit Spaniens berühmtester Illustrator. Er studierte an der Industrial Mastery School und der Hochschule für angewandte Künste in Zaragoza technische Zeichnungen, Malerei, Deko und Innengestaltung. Zunächst als Maler, Comiczeichner und Designer tätig, begann er sich 1983 als Illustrator zu betätigen und beginnt schließlich seine Karriere als weltweit anerkannter und populärer Künstler für Verlage in USA, England, Schweden, natürlich Spanien und vielen weiteren Ländern. Seine Arbeiten wurden in allen möglichen Publikationen sowohl auf nationaler als auch auf internationaler Ebene veröffentlicht. "Heavy Metal", "National Lampoon" oder "Cimoc" seien hier exemplarisch genannt. Zu seinen zahlreichen Auftraggebern gehörten u.a. Tor Books, Berkley Books, Avon, Warner Books, Bantam Books, etc.

Ab 199o beginnt er, seine Auftragsarbeiten in Büchern zu veröffentlichen, die darüberhinaus Werke enthalten, die exklusiv nur für diese Bücher kreiert wurden.

Im gleichen Jahr erscheint "Women", und es dürfte nicht schwerfallen, zu erraten, was im Mittelpunkt dieser Publikation steht: die Überfrau in allen denkbaren Facetten. Später folgen "Malefic", in den eine andere seiner Obsessionen auftaucht: das Thema der Schönen und des Biests, "Secrets", "III Millennium" (seine persönliche Vision zum Ende des Jahrtausends), "Dreams" und schließlich "Prohibited Book". Darüberhinaus schuf er auch Cover für Bücher, Videospiele, Kalender, Zeitschriften, usw. Außerdem wurden verschiedene Kartenspiele mit seinen phantastischen Illustrationen veröffentlicht, so z.B. das "Black Tarot". 1996 gewinnt er den Silberpreis Spectrum III: Das Beste an zeitgenössischer fantastischer Kunst, einer von mehreren Preisen in Royos Leben.

Inzwischen sind Royos Arbeiten in vielfältiger Gestalt erhältlich, darunter Kalender, Poster, T-Shirts, CD-Cover, Mouse-Pads, und vieles mehr.

Luis Royo wird Skulpteur

Luis Royo ist nicht nur ein großartiger Illustrator und Zeichner. Wir konnten auch schon einen flüchtigen Blick auf seine fantastischen Wortwelten erhaschen, die seine Bücher ausschmücken. Und nun können wir auch bald seine Skulpturen bewundern. Geleitet von einem unstillbaren Durst, neue Welten zu entdecken, hat Royo mit der Arbeit an einer gewaltigen Skulptur begonnen: die Büste des berühmten Mädchens mit der Metalldornenkrone. Zum Zeitpunkt des Redaktionsschlusses von Art Fantastix #2 wurde seine Schöpfung lediglich beim International Airbrush Forum '99 in Castrop-Rauxel der Öffentlichkeit präsentiert. Die weltwichtigste Airbrush-Messe widmete die Ausstellung der letztjährigen Messe Luis Royo und zeigte die Skulptur als Hauptattraktion. Die Büste ist ziemlich groß, und es wird angedacht, eine kleine Zahl von Staturen für den Verkauf zu produzieren.

Luis Royo klingt gut

Nein, Luis Royo startet keine Karriere als Musiker. Neben Novellen, Videospielen und Filmen, gestaltete er auch CD-Cover, insbesondere für Hardrock-Bands, und so kann man heute Royos Kunst also auch in den Musikgeschäften weltweit bewundern. Gute Beispiele hierfür sind die Bands "Belzebú" (Türkei), "Zeitreisen" (Deutschland) oder "Black Flight" (Frankreich). Letztere waren wirklich originell und ließen gleich mehrere Royo-Motive als Cover für die gleiche CD proudzieren. Darüberhinaus bekam die CD statt der gewöhnlichen runden Form, die Form des jeweiligen Kunstwerks. Das Ergebnis war wirklich sehenswert.

Sein Beiträge: Art Fantastix #2 **und** Art Fantastix Platinum #1

Bibliographie

BILDBÄNDE

- Art Fantastix #2: The Art of Luis Royo
  Der einzigartige Bildband bietet einen Querschnitt durch alle Werke Luis Royos.

- Art Fantastix Platinum #1: The Art of Luis Royo
  Dieser Band ist ein Remake des vergriffenen Art Fantastix #2.

- Dreams
  Dreams ist - sowohl chronologisch als auch thematisch - eine umfassende Reise durch die Karriere des spanischen Autors. Sie beinhaltet alle Auftragsarbeiten von Royo der letzten zehn Jahre. Ein gemischtes Kompendium, in dem er seine unbestreitbare Vielseitigkeit unter Beweis stellt.

- III Millennium
  Das dritte Jahrtausend als Aufhänger nutzend, schafft Royo seinen wohl futuristischsten Bildband - voll von High-Tech-Elementen, aber auch angereichert mit Dekadenz. Kalte Landschaften und apokalyptische Ruinen einer Zukunft, die viel schlimmer ist, als die Gegenwart, sind die Normalität in diesem beunruhigenden Buch.

- Malefic
  In Malefic präsentiert Royo die dunkelste und wildeste Seite seiner Werke. Fantasy und Science-Fiction dominieren einmal mehr seine Werke, in einem Bildband, der zum allerersten Mal Skizzen und Kommentare des Autors zu all seinen Illustrationen beinhaltet.

- Prohibited Book
  Prohibited Book, der provokativste von Luis Royos Bildbänden, erschient im November 1999. Der Künstler hat seine ursprünglichsten Instinkten freien Lauf gelassen, seinen niedersten Leidenschaften, seinen verborgenen Begierden. Ein überraschendes Buch, das den Leser von der ersten Seite an schockt; und das mit einer Stärke, wie sie nur ein sündiger Autor vermitteln kann.

- Puuf of Devils

- Secrets
  Luis Royos Kunst ist grenzenlos in ihrer Entwicklung, und das wird in diesem Band belegt, wo er eine zermürbende, dunkle Welt mit den schönsten Nymphen Seite an Seite mit den gräßlichsten Kreaturen präsentiert und dabei ein Bild jenseits rein künstlerischer Konzeption schafft.

- Women
  Dies ist der erste von Royos Bildbänden, doch schon hier erkennt man einen ausgereiften Illustrator erkennen, der in der Lage ist, seine Kunst in jedes Genre zu übertragen. Die weiblichen Formen, die in folgenden Werken eine fast absolute Dominanz erreichen, treten hier zum ersten Mal in Erscheinung.

COMICALBEN

- Circulus-Sataka

- Desfase

TRADING CARD SETS

- Artist's Choice
  (zusammen mit anderen Künstlern)

- Forbidden Universe

- From Fantasy to Reality
  (zusammen mit anderen Künstlern)

- Millennium

- Secret Desires

- The Art of Heavy Metal

- The Best of Royo

PORTFOLIOS

- III Millennium

- Tattoos

- Warm Winds

ANDERES

- Poster
  (Diverse Motive)

- The Black Tarot
  (mit 78 Karten)

- Striptease Postcard Collection #1
  (mit 10 Postkarten)

Born in 1945 in Olalla, a small town in Teruel. Soon afterwards he moved with his family to Zaragoza, where he went to his first school, and where his first memories come from, with drawing already playing a major part. In his first memory, he is sitting in front of the large school windows, and tracing the drawings that his teacher gave him.

His practical side, which he acquired from his family, led him to study Technical Drawing for Construction. He soon discovered that geometric forms did not completely satisfy him.

He began to study painting, decoration and interior design in the Industrial School and the School of Applied Arts, and he combined this with different jobs in interior design and decoration studios in 1970 and 1971.

During this time he also combined his employment activity with painting. Influenced by May ´68 he made large format paintings with social themes, which he exhibited in group shows between 1972 and 1976, followed by a series of individual exhibitions in 1977.

On discovering adult comics with the work of artists such as Enki Bilal and Moebius, in 1978 he began to draw comic strips for different fanzines and he exhibited in the in 1980.

In 1979 he left his jobs in the decoration studios, despite being father to a son, to dedicate himself entirely to comics. In 1981 and 1982 his work was published in magazines such as 1984, Comix international, Rambla and, occasionally, in El Víbora and Heavy Metal.

A meeting in 1983 with 1983 con Rafael Martínez, in the Zaragoza Comic Fair would establish his professional future. He was commissioned by Martinez to produce five illustrations for Norma Editorial marking the start of a professional relationship which still thrives today.

The first commissions came straight away. His work was no longer restricted to national territory and was frequently published in the foreign media. Among other countries he has published work in the USA, Great Britain and Sweden, as well as producing cover illustrations for prestigious publishing houses such as Tor Books, Berkley Books, Avon, Warner Books, Batman Books and others.

American magazines such as Heavy Metal and National Lampoon often turned to Luis Royo for their cover illustrations, as well European magazines like Cimoc, Comic Art, Ere Comprime, Total Metal and others. However, his work was not just restricted to magazine covers as he was also asked to make covers for videos and computer games.

In 1985, parallel to his work as an illustrator, he published a comic album in the Rambla series and a year later Ikusager Ediciones S.A. published an experimental comic by him entitled DESFASE.

From 1990, once established in a privileged position in the international illustration market, he expanded the production of his own work, as opposed to commissioned works. Most of his own work was bought by different media or included in compilation works.

In 1992, following a proposal a few years earlier by the man who, nine years ago, had discovered him as an illustrator, he published his first compilation work: WOMEN - an album which brought together his best illustrations to date. With this book he was already recognised as a great illustrator and his preference for drawing the female figure began to emerge clearly. It was a surprising book for comic lovers, covering a series of different genres, which led to its publication by Editorial Soleil in France and Ediciones Comic Forum in Germany. On the basis of this compilation he undertook his first exhibition of original illustrations.

A year later, Comic Images brought out a collection of Trading Cards using his illustrations, under the title FROM FANTASY TO REALITY.

Following the success of the first compilation, in 1994 MALEFIC was published in with most of the illustrations by Luis Royo, establishing a different world and range of colours. In MALEFIC the whole illustrator was revealed - an illustrator capable not only of portraying fantasy worlds, but also of creating a story and a sculpture around the character who gives the book its title.

In the same year, WOMEN was republished, and in the USA Penthouse ran an article on his illustrations.

In 1995, new publishers began to take an interest in the work of Luis Royo: Ballantine, Nal, Daw, Doubleday, Harper Paperbacks, Zebra, Fasa Corporation, Pocket Books for the Star Trek series, Penthouse Comix and Fller Ultra X-Men by Marvel. From that year on, the work of Luis Royo appears in many different formats, in different countries (including Eastern European countries): calendars, posters, T-shirts, CD covers, mouse mats, Trading Card collections in collaboration with other artists, such as THE ART OF HEAVY METAL or individually, in the case of his third collecting of trading cards, THE BEST OF ROYO.

The fantasy and quality of Luis Royo's work began to find its place in all kinds of media, and his name became increasingly well known. In 1996 he had a Penthouse cover in USA and Germany, along with an article in the magazine. The same year many reports about his work appeared in prestigious publications including La Stampa in Italy, Airbrush Action in USA and Germany, and in Penthouse Comix. He also received the Silver Award SPECTRUM III the best in contemporary Fantastic Art in the USA.

Following on from MALEFIC, his third album, SECRETS, appeared in 1996 with magic and the female figure occupying the central roles, with the underlying presence of the fairytale Beauty and the Beast. This work was published by NBM for English-speaking countries. But there were yet more surprises to come that year for his fans with the WARM WINDS portfolio, published by Norma Editorial in cooperation with Heavy Metal.

In 1997, Heavy Metal's interest in Luis Royo was reflected in a host of covers and calendars, as well as in its Gallery, which was entirely dedicated to Royo. This interest culminated in a commission for the cover of the 20th anniversary edition of the magazine and a series of illustrations on the F.A.A.K. character (Julie Strain) by Kevin Eastman.

That same year, Comic Images brought our two new collections of Trading Cards: ROYO SECRET DESIRES (the fourth individual collection by the artist) and ARTISTIC CHOICES (jointly with other artists). To end the year WOMEN and MALEFIC were published in the USA and the latter was republished in Spain.

A year later, the next book of illustrations appeared: III MILENIUM. In this book, Royo renews his palette of colours and gives us his own particular vision of the end of the century. Also in 1998 he presented his collection of Tarot Cards, THE BLACK TAROT (for which he designed new images and a personalised view of the symbolism of the cards). In 1999 he produced the Heavy Metal calendar and his fifth collection of Trading Cards under the III MILENIUM name. It was a year in which Luis Royo displayed a clear evolution towards a much more intimate and daring style of illustration.

To coincide with the Barcelona Comic Fair in 1999, Royo presented a new album: DREAMS - a compilation of all the commissioned illustrations of the previous ten years. What stands out most in this album is the versatility with which the artist is able to adapt to different subjects and styles. The first vinyl figure based on these illustrations (on the cover of MALEFIC) was produced by Inteleg in 1999, and supervised by the artist himself.

The artist offered us a new twist at the end of the year with work that was more daring and honest than ever before: the publication of the first volume of the PROHIBITED BOOK, with a surprising erotic content in which the tale of Beauty and the Beast takes on a major importance. This deluxe publication, smaller than the previous albums, offers images which are as sensual as they are elegant.

EVOLUTION takes us back to the large format album, combining more personal works with commissions. The selection of illustrations are marked by the hands of the clock, times past and science fiction are represented in the omnipresent female figure, whose expression has become more confident and dominant. This album is accompanied by a study of the MALEFIC character.

Originally conceived as a trilogy, PROHIBITED BOOK II was published in 2001 - a book in which sensations are transferred to the reader through the strength of the characters. In continuity with the first volume, we are offered a different view of sensuality, closer to forbidden dreams and secret desires.

Concentrating increasingly on his personal work, his best illustrations of women would be reproduced by Fournier in a pack of poker cards.

In 2002, Luis Royo revealed some of his secrets in CONCEPTIONS - a book which describes the creative process and presents a collection of the artist's sketches and pencil drawings, allowing us to enjoy the character studies, the conception of the illustrations and the numerous alternatives which Royo considers before carrying out the definitive work.

VISIONS was published in 2003. It is a compilation with an introduction by Kevin Eastman, creator of the Teenage Mutant Ninja Turtles, in which the images are dominated by fantasy and the Luis Royo's creative talent develops new details and a broader palette of colours, with the incorporation if dragons who occupy a privileged position together with the ever-present female figure.

PROHIBITED BOOK III was the last in the Prohibited Book series. In this volume, the reader becomes trapped in images of beauty, tenderness and desire - images in which sensuality can even be seen as a monster.
At the end of 2003 the artist opened up his work with a series of sketches and drafts for the illustrations in his compilation albums, accompanied by texts to enrich the reader's experience and provide a greater understanding of his method. CONCEPTIONS II goes further than the first volume by introducing colour, with colour drawings to contrast with the pencil sketches.

FANTASTIC ART is the major compilation to date. Published in May 2004 it brings together the most complete collection of illustrations by the artist. Published in two high quality formats, the limited deluxe edition is a good example of the importance of the compilation. Fantasy and reality come together through images in which Royo presents his own particular view of the world, of the myths and legends which have shaped it over time. It is a cosmogonist vision of reality where the future has to assume its own challenges.

Luis Royo moved to Barcelona, where he found a corner bursting with beauty in the Gothic Quarter, in which to create his work. This change in residence also meant a change in the way he worked, in his vision of his work and a desire to return to painting on canvas, to move towards more personal work which would once again surprise the reader.

PROHIBITED SKETCHBOOK is the latest work published by the artist. In it we can enjoy the sensuality and colourless desire of the Prohibited book in its initial stages. It includes original sketches in which the strength of the images is already evident. As a special lure, it includes sketches of illustrations which, despite their incredible force, do not appear in previous publications.

In his latest period, in combination with other work, Luis Royo has spent four years developing one of his most personal works - THE LABYRINTH: TAROT. This tarot card design displays the limitless perfectionism of the artist. It is a pack in which every image has been carefully studied and which demonstrates a titanic level of documentation.

THE LABYRINTH: TAROT is the first completely unpublished work by Luis Royo, where not one of the images has been previously published. It will be published in December 2004 in two formats: an exclusive pack of cards and a book including all the illustrations together with explanatory texts, written by the artist himself, on the hidden meaning of each card and their power over people's destiny.

Since he began working as an illustrator, many Heavy Metal groups from different countries (Germany, Italy, Spain, etc.) have adopted the drawings of Luis Royo, using them for their CD and record covers. Among his most recent works are the two latest CDs of the Austrian group, Avalanch.

We are clearly talking about one of the most successful international illustrators, whose fame - rather than distancing him - has led him to a permanent process of searching for new challenges and proposals, experimenting with colour, texture and even finding new forms of expression outside illustration. He is a tireless worker who has made fans all over the world, with a magical fantasy vision of everything that surrounds him, experimenting and evolving, and justifying his privileged position in the international illustration market

On September 27th, 1998, the newspaper El Periódico de Aragón published a double page with this interview, one of the most interesting ones published ever with the author.
Tell me about your beginnings...

I was born in Cutanda, and my parents were emigrants. I was taken here when I was six months old, so I have barely lived in a village, except for the summers, when I stayed with my grandparents. My story is the usual one. I liked painting a lot when I was a child, and my mother always told me: "My son, make something useful, painters usually starve to death." I studied to be a building draughtsman, and then I went on to decoration, because I thought it was more artistic. I attended to some painting courses in the Art School and worked in decoration studies for eight years. But I was already making comics, attending exhibitions, painting at home...

What kind of painting did you make?

It was a painting typical at the time, with large formats. Social painting, criticizing Franco, the police, etc. Everything was very grim (maybe a cop's head with a Popeye can, that kind of painting), following the style of Equipo Crónica or Rafael Canogar.

And from 1978 on, you chose the field of comics. Who and what persuaded you to undergo that radical change?

It was probably the Totem magazine, and the comic style that came after May '68. It was like a revelation. Until that moment, I had only seen things such as Roberto Alcázar y Pedrín.

So I began making comic books, and all of a sudden I left decoration behind; it was a kind of suicide, because I locked myself at home for two or three years. I drew a lot of comic pages, something that, seen from my current point of view, seems really crazy. I had no idea how the world of comics did work, but I created a huge amount of work, grabbed a folder and went to France, which, in theory, was the birthplace of comic. The companies at Paris accepted some of my works, but not many, specially when compared to the great quantity I had made. I made surrealist books, based on some weird scripts by Antonio Altarriba.

How did you make the leap? I read in your biography that from 1981 on, you began collaborating with many publications: El Víbora, Rambla...

Yeah, it was a very important change because this way I could publish my work quite often. All of a sudden, I realized that repeating a character in each different panel was very tedious for me, and I couldn't stand it. So I took another radical turn and started making illustrations. That's where I feel most comfortable, and I'm still on it. I am a creator of imaginary worlds, who works in two directions: one thing is a commissioned work and another, completely different, is my own freedom as a creator, the few albums I make for myself. And I still retain this freedom. At the end of the day, when I am finishing a book such as III Millennium, I always tell my agent not to call me in the following two months. It is too dangerous to shut up everything of a sudden, because this trickle of commissioned works is also a kind of awakening, a call towards risk and challenge, and also towards self-healing. For me, documentation is basic. I get ideas from fashion magazines, from cinema, from classic art. An artist is like an sponge. Occasionally, I sit down, put on my headphones and listen to some music clips, by Prince or other people. And I get a lot of ideas from this, too.

I have paid particular attention to your technique, so elaborate and perfect, dazzling, photographic, the hyper-realism of dream. Can you explain us how do you do this?

I use a lot of materials. Many times I begin with water colors, other times with acrylics, even others with pencils... I use the airbrush gradually, discovering the illustration step by step. At the end, when you have the whole composition, and the figure is more or less perfect, you must use oil to finish it completely. The oil's richness in color is much higher than that of acrylics, water colors or any other material.

What about your fascination about women and their uninhibited anatomy: beautiful eyes, faces, breasts, pubis, buttocks. Isn't it a bit sick?

I'm being sincere: if you are the kind of man who like women a lot, any time you idealize a character, a woman will come to your mind. I also draw men. But the woman is the being I like the most. Even if I think about the fallen angel and Lucifer's iconography, I always add some women angels inevitably. Nakedness is one of the canons of beauty, but I do not always paint naked women. Our civilization is changing very quickly, and our taste for women is changing too. It is not the same the kind of androgynous woman from the end of the eighties, who practiced body-building, had a strong gaze and, on the other hand, was more innocent, than the archetype of nowadays, sicker but also wicker. Those women who are fashionable at the moment have a certain "junkie" look, with a skeletal, bony body, such as Kate Moss. They say that the next step will be towards a more normal type, such as Nieves Álvarez. I don't think so, because I think there is not much perversion in the norm, and everything has a point of perversion, strangeness. That's the reason I insist so much on the issue of the Beauty and the Beast. I'm sure that the human being is full of dark corners, that at heart, all of us are mental perverts. We don't even want to look inside ourselves.

Is this perception of the hidden, what fascinates so much American people?

American society is completely sick and puritan, and the Clinton-Lewinsky case has proven it again. But here we are following the same path... All the countries have their peculiarities: American people feel disturbed in front of sex, but the Germans cannot stand the sight of blood. They have censored some of my illustrations.

You seem to fight Puritanism with glamour, beauty and provocation, bestialism and zoophilia.

I punish them as much as I can. In III Millennium there is a black Christ. And my last work, Prohibited Book, has a strong sexual character, including homosexual scenes, zoophilia, old photographs...
They say Aragonese people do not have imagination... You are the exception.

What would Luis Buñuel have said? Let's be serious. My whole world of dreams is very important. I have live locked in my house, but this can become a real obsession. All of a sudden, I realize that I must go down to El Corte Inglés, if only to be pulled, pushed, to go upstairs and downstairs, to feel that I live in a city, with people around me, to know that I belong to this world, because at the end of the day, I can believe only in what I see in my drawing board. And I am not joking. From time to time, I have a real identity problem. Who am I? Am I living inside the drawing board?

I was told in the Taj Mahal bookstore that, when you feel inspired, you don't even shave nor get a shower.

That's what I said when I presented a book of mine. Now I have been educated a bit more by my wife. Today I have taken a shower, but maybe I hadn't taken one for a whole week because I was too involved in a project. When I get too involved in a book, it's like when you are hunting. I even try to avoid any reading so as to not loose concentration.

But you sleep, don't you?

Yes, there was a time when I got to bed dressed, so as to not change my clothes. Everybody has a certain sickness: I am a pessimistic, tending to depression, and I need the maximum concentration. I had to take everything out of my mind: I didn't open the windows, I didn't go out, I didn't change my clothes until I finished a work. When you work, you commune with it, you put your five senses on it. I felt I had to do it that way, and that's how I did it. I spent whole nights working, going to bed at four a.m., with my clothes and shoes on, and then later I got up and went back to work. Maybe it was a lack of method. I suffered much more than now. Now I suffer too, because I create my works with pain and suffering, with obsession and pleasure, but it's not so hard as before. When I am finishing an art book, I don't leave my house for two months. And I only get a shower once in a while.

I don't know if I should ask this question...

Do I make love those days? Of course not. Really.

And this violent background in your work, is it a kind of criticism, an apology, or just one of your preoccupations?

What really annoys me is this pure society, so prudish, that feels disturbed in front of sex and violence. For me, it is so disagreeable and false that they feel attracted to my illustrations, which are natural. I think I couldn't kill a fly. But I like to provoke, to disturb.

Do you mean you do an apology of violence with your work?

Yes, and I don't care to admit it. We have an inner violence, and I think that negating it does not make sense. Guide it, control yourself. To negate it is like going to the Prado Museum and taking away all the pictures including violent scenes. Only a few Dutch landscapes would be left. You can go the Sistine Chapel and see a lot of demons there, as well as naked bodies, and an explosive sexuality. Then, suddenly, we are in the twentieth century and we are saying that violence and television, damage children... What I think is harmful in TV is all those shows of lewdness, all those people explaining their distresses, that we can see now in any channel. Let them dream. Children love violence, that's what keeps them alive. When my son was younger, I took him to watch any kind of movies, or I scared the hell out of him with horror tales, and I think that was very interesting... These kind of attitudes are very disagreeable for me. Now they want to play classic music to children. Come on! You need to hit them hard so their heads get full of images. This will configure a beautiful inner world. But beware, to pick up a gun is a completely different thing. From a strictly creative point of view, violence, like evil, is very useful, and the creator needs them. Without it, you could not understand history, civilization or even humanity as a whole.

Behind a winner there is always a resented. Do you feel mistreated here?

Yes, a little bit, but it does not hurt me. There was a time when I felt more pain, and I felt very bad. You go outside, where your work is appreciated and exhibited, and then you come back from the United States, full of illusion, and nobody tells you anything. Often, I think that people in charge of culture in this area are still living in the Transition, are stagnant.

They don't have agility. When I travel abroad, I see that industry supports culture everywhere. Here, everything seems focused toward retired elder people (and I don't have anything against them).

Yes, but they are recovering a very interesting patrimony.

Don't exaggerate. There is a museum of illustration in Massachusetts, and some of my works are exhibited there. In Germany too. These are places which are modern, agile, interesting for young people. Here, the institutions' gearing is antiquated, and those people have out-of-fashion ideas. Culture in Aragon is too old-fashioned. I have always loved Barcelona, I would need three lives to see all that city can offer. There was a moment when it seemed that here we were reaching the same level as Barcelona, but now the distance between both cities is huge again.

You cannot complain. You are the living proof that Zaragoza can triumph outside Spain.

I am not complaining. Things are being very good for me. Now the only things you need is a fax, your agent and your work. Two days later, my work is being exhibited in New York. What else can I ask?

Let's talk about your tastes.

I read few novels, and often because of professional reasons. There are works that take two weeks to complete. I must read so much documentation! Time is the biggest tyrant of this end of century. I love boxing, is the most plastic sport in the world.

I have seen in your books that you quote Dante, John Milton, Tolkien...

I read from the classics to the Latin American, all I can grab and is demanded by my profession. I do not read many newspapers, and do not watch news in TV. I am an image-consumer. I never see any TV series.

Do you feel definitely Aragonese?

Yes, yes, but I am not fond of regionalisms. I am a citizen of the world. I think that being Aragonese is just having been born in one specific place. I was born here and I feel good here.

WOMEN

This is the first of Royo's art-books, but we can already see a full-fledged illustrator, able to adapt his art to any genre. The feminine figure, which in future works will attain an almost absolute prominence, is beginning to emerge in this book .

MALEFIC

In Malefic, Royo presents the darkest, wildest side of his creations. Fantasy and science-fiction again predominate in his works, in an art-book that, for the first time ever, includes sketches and author comments on all of the illustrations.

SECRETS

Luis Royo's art is boundless in its evolution, and this is proved in Secrets, where he presents an unnerving, dark world with the most beautiful nymphs siding with the most hideous creatures, creating an image beyond pure artistic conception.

III MILLENNIUM

Using the upcoming third millennium as an excuse, Royo creates his most futuristic art-book, full of high-tech elements, but also filled with decadence. Cold landscapes and apocalyptic ruins in a future far worse than the present are the norm in this disturbing book.

DREAMS

Dreams is an comprehensive journey, both chronological and thematic, throughout the Spanish author's career. It gathers all the commissioned works made by Royo for the last ten years. A heterogeneous compendium where he proves his undeniable versatility.

PROHIBITED BOOK

Prohibited Book has always been Luis Royo's most challenging books. Here, the writer has been lured by the lowest instincts, the most unbridled passions and the darkest desires. It is a surprising book that shakes the reader from the very first page with a force that only this transgressive artist can transmit.

EVOLUTION

A definitive journey by all those topics that really interest Luis Royo, from King Arthur to future societies, Evolution mixes the spell of demonic beauties with the monstrous beasts. These pages gather not only ordered works which have illustrated novels all over the world but also original creations full of fantasy and mystery.

PROHIBITED BOOK 2

This new part about the artist's darkest desires explores fantasies stemming not from the world of flesh and sheer physical relation, but from the world of imagination. This picture collection is the perfect complement for the dreams hinted in the first volume.

CONCEPTIONS

From the idea of a travel book which gathers the whole creation process of a picture, this volume is a collection of sketches and pictures made with pencils that bear witness to the high quality of Luis Royo as a creative artist, with works that go from chivalry genre to witchery.